Ninety-Nine Words for Rain

(and One for Sun)

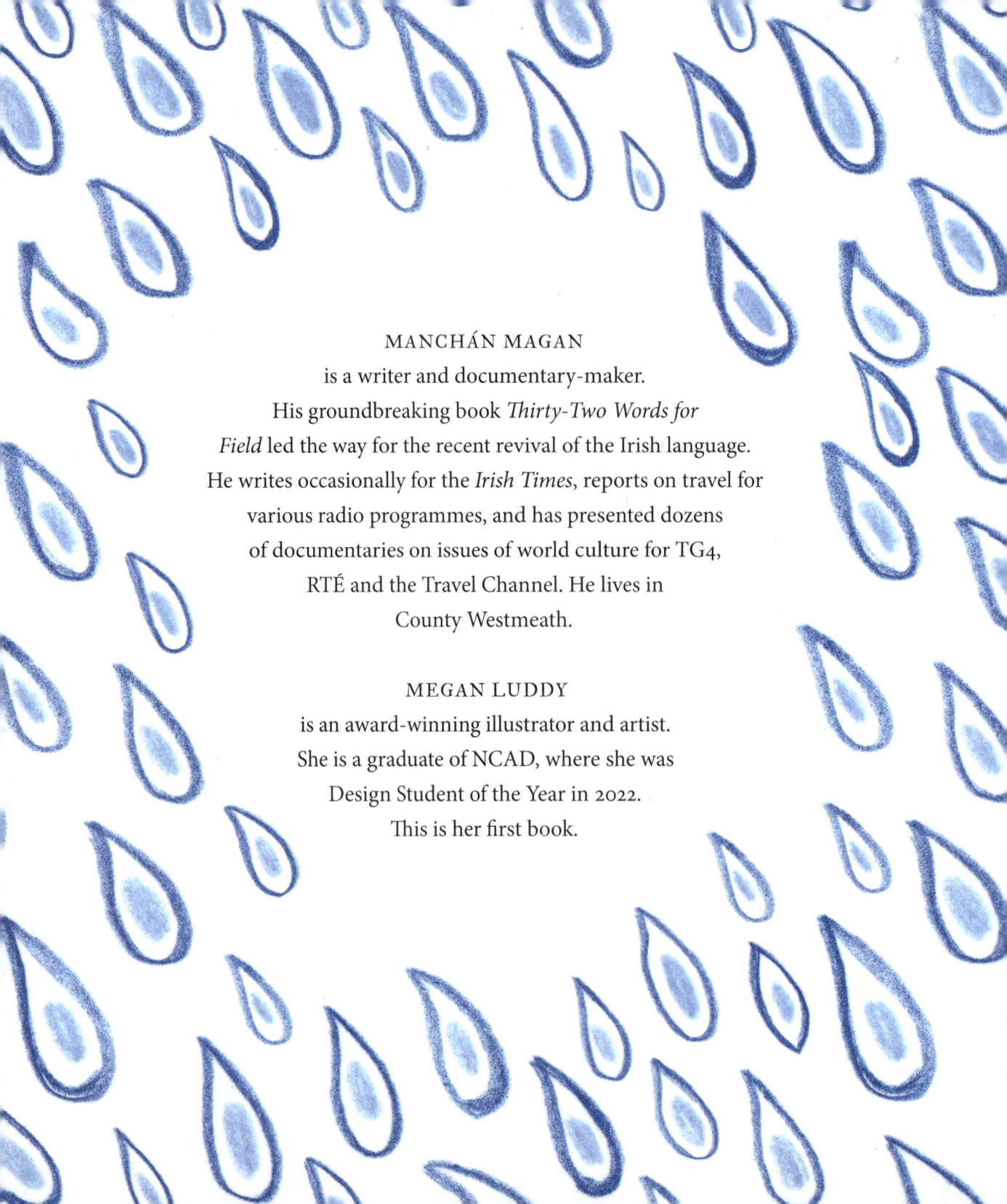

MANCHÁN MAGAN
is a writer and documentary-maker.
His groundbreaking book *Thirty-Two Words for Field* led the way for the recent revival of the Irish language. He writes occasionally for the *Irish Times*, reports on travel for various radio programmes, and has presented dozens of documentaries on issues of world culture for TG4, RTÉ and the Travel Channel. He lives in County Westmeath.

MEGAN LUDDY
is an award-winning illustrator and artist.
She is a graduate of NCAD, where she was
Design Student of the Year in 2022.
This is her first book.

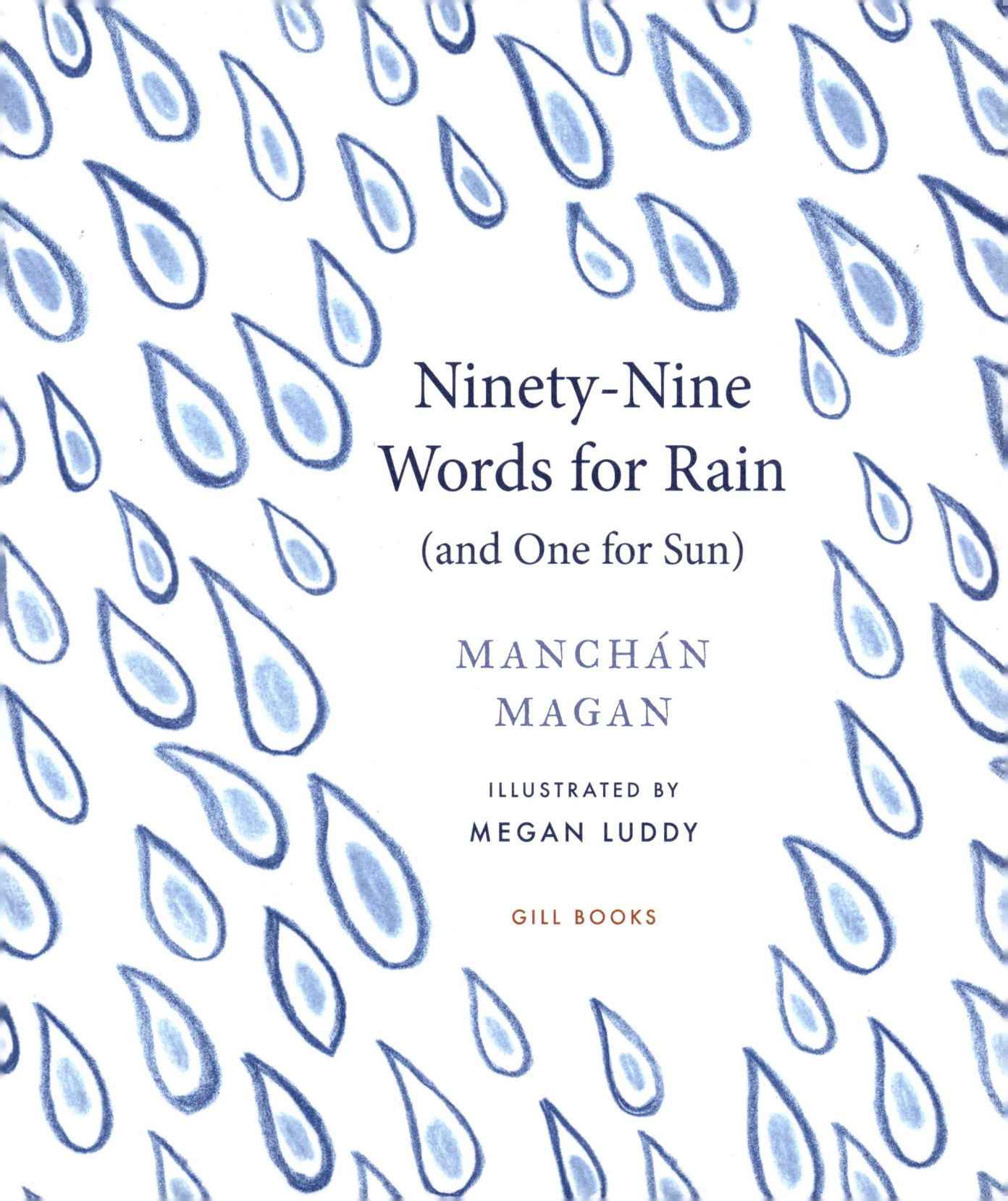

Ninety-Nine Words for Rain
(and One for Sun)

MANCHÁN MAGAN

ILLUSTRATED BY
MEGAN LUDDY

GILL BOOKS

Gill Books
Hume Avenue
Park West
Dublin 12
www.gillbooks.ie

Gill Books is an imprint of M.H. Gill and Co.

Text © Manchán Magan 2025
Illustrations © Megan Luddy 2025

9781804583340

Designed by Graham Thew © Gill Books
Edited by Ruairí Ó Brógáin
Proofread by Anna Kealy
Printed and bound by Firmengruppe APPL, Germany
This book is typeset in Minion Pro.

The paper used in this book comes from the wood pulp of sustainably managed forests.

All rights reserved.
No part of this publication may be copied, reproduced or transmitted in any form or by any means, without written permission of the publishers.

To the best of our knowledge, this book complies in full with the requirements of the General Product Safety Regulation (GPSR). For further information and help with any safety queries, please contact us at productsafety@gill.ie.

A CIP catalogue record for this book is available from the British Library.

5 4 3

Introduction

THE PROVERB *is maith an scéalaí an aimsir* ('Weather is a good storyteller') is true on so many levels. Weather is a continuous story generator, offering insights, anecdotes and fresh narratives for us to celebrate, bemoan, connect with and commiserate over on a daily, and even hourly, basis.

There are other ways too in which weather is a *scéalaí* ('storyteller'), such as how references to storms, floods and droughts in the old mythological tales and historical accounts give us insights into life long ago. The words used to describe the weather conditions can be especially helpful in bridging the gap between us and our forebears.

This little book is a celebration of these words and an exploration of how those who came before us were able to observe and describe the specific characteristics of every form of meteorological experience, from hoar frost to heat haze. It's an attempt to reach back in time to connect with them and to reflect not only on the climatic conditions they endured and enjoyed but also on how their experiences impact us today, in an era of climate change.

Some words and phrases offer an almost choreographic description of our reaction to weather, such as that for a cold morning, *maidin le bheith ag pógadh na gcopán* (literally, 'a morning to be kissing the kneecaps', summoning an image of staying underneath the covers with your knees tucked up underneath your chin), or *gaoth a bhainfeadh an craiceann d'fhíogach* ('wind that would skin a dogfish', in reference to a harsh east wind). Others manage to capture the uniquely unpredictable and capricious quality of Irish weather, such as *lá na seacht síon, le gaoth mhór, báisteach, sioc agus sneachta, tintreach, tóirneach agus lonrú gréine* ('a day of seven weathers, with high wind, rain, frost and snow, thunder, lightning and sunshine'). A surprising number of days in Ireland can be described in these terms.

*

Each of the rain words gathered here likely arose from countless sodden, shivery experiences on this Atlantic-swept island of ours. Reading them offers a visceral sense of what the generations that preceded us endured in a world without Gore-Tex or central heating. The writer Frank McCourt is sometimes lampooned for his fixation on the wetness of his Limerick childhood in the memoir *Angela's Ashes*, and yet the multitude of terms our people amassed suggests he may actually have downplayed the ubiquitousness of *báisteach fadó* ('rain long ago').

Researching and collating this litany of weather words has left me with a compassion for, and a closeness to, those who coined the terms. Without their fortitude and their ability to endure the downpours, it's possible that we wouldn't be here today.

Some of the terms were likely created by the weather specialists of their era: the *néaladóirí* (cloud-watchers), *réadóirí* (stargazers) and *fiachairí* (those who observe ravens for signs of weather change). The closeness with which they observed every advancing cloud and pressure front is evident from the sheer richness and variety of terms they amassed.

There may not have been the sophisticated technology of today, but our forebears were skilled at reading the signs of birds, trees, animals, insects and fish, as well as markers on land and sea. Birds were particularly good forecasters: swallows flying low foretold rain, as did hens roosting early, curlews calling, ducks loudly quacking and seagulls seen far inland. The heron's behaviour offered many hints: *Aimsir chrua thirim nuair a bhíonn an corr éisc suas in aghaidh srutha chun na sléibhte* ('When the heron flies upstream to the mountains, the weather will be dry but rough') and *Fearthainn nuair a thagann sí an abhainn anuas* ('When she goes downstream, it will rain').

Robins too could offer insights, depending on where they were and how good you were at observing their behaviour. *Má bhíonn an spideog faoi thor ar maidin, beidh sé ina lá fliuch* ('If a robin hides beneath a bush in the morning, rain is on the way'). If you see them high in the trees, it means something else: *Dea-shíon an spideog ar bharr na gcrann* ('Good weather when the robin is high on the branches').

Plants also offered signs, for those who knew how to look: clover leaves closing up meant impending rain, while a heavy crop of haws meant a harsh winter, as did leaves withering too quickly in autumn.

*

Weather lore was an area of focus of the Irish Folklore Commission, established in the 1930s to collect the traditional knowledge of communities throughout the 26 counties of the Irish Free State. Between 1937 and 1939, fifty thousand schoolchildren from five thousand schools gathered folklore from their elders in a project known as the Schools' Collection (Bailiúchán na Scol). Among the myriad topics covered were signs of good or bad weather, predictions based on the appearance of the sky, moon-related weather lore, animal behaviour as weather indicators, plant-related weather signs and traditional methods of weather forecasting.

On the Aran Islands, for example, the schoolchildren recorded that good weather was expected *nuair a thagann an rón i ngar don talamh* ('when the seal approaches the land'), *nuair a bhíonn torann mór ag an bhfarraige* ('when there's a loud noise from the sea') and *nuair a bhíonn dath nádúrtha ar an bhfarraige* ('when the sea has a natural hue to it').

Auguries of rain included *dath gorm a bheith ar an bhfarraige* ('the sea appearing blue'), *an rón ag dul i bhfad amach ins an bhfarraige* ('the seal going far out to sea'), *an trá a bheith bog* ('the strand being soft') and *an talamh ó thuaidh a bheith i ngar* ('the land to the north appearing near').

There were so many different signs that could predict weather recorded throughout the country that it's hard to do them justice here. A cat, for example, could reveal impending rain if it lay with its back to the fire, while its scratching the leg of a table or chair signalled a storm. If it washed its face before the fire, good weather could be expected, but crossing its paws meant a flood within three days. Dogs too were said to be forecasters: if they ate grass, it was a sign of fine weather; but if they drank water from a spring, bad weather was due.

In fact, most animals were thought to be able to reveal some aspect of impending weather. Pigs were believed to be able to see the wind, and so a pig staring closely ahead indicated a storm brewing. The same conclusion could be drawn from sheep gathering into valleys or huddling by fences. Yet when sheep, goats or cows were seen grazing on the hilltops, it meant fine weather.

Even insects could predict the future. A spider retreating to the edges of its web was a sign of clement weather, while pond skaters out in great numbers meant rain. Children would keep 'water flies' in a jar as a type of barometer. Since the presence of midges and flies were also predictors of rain, it's no wonder that the sight of fish jumping for them was too.

The elements of weather lore that come closest to modern meteorology are those to do with the sun and moon. In the folklore of every county it's recorded that rain is due if a ring is seen around a pale moon. This is still widely mentioned in my home community in County Westmeath. The wider the ring, the nearer the rain. The idea is contained within the expression *súil circe ré* ('the moon of the hen's eye') and in the proverb *Garraí na gealaí, báisteach* ('A garden around the moon means rain'). It's also expressed as *Tá lios ar an ngealach* ('There's a fairy fort on the moon'). This belief aligns with the fact that cirrus clouds, which can create halos, often precede low-pressure systems, bringing rain. The clarity of the visual phenomenon known as the Man in the Moon (created by the moon's volcanic plains contrasting with the brighter, cratered highlands) was also a sign of impending rain. The other reference to the moon that I hear frequently among neighbours is that if the moon appears to be lying on its back, bad weather will follow.

As in most cultures in the world, the sun was portrayed as a god of the heavens in Ireland before the arrival of St Patrick, and it was thought to lie down to sleep in the evening. Its rays were thought to be its legs, which accounts for the expression *Togha na haimsire chughainn – cosa na gréine suas ar maidin agus síos trathnóna* ('The best of weather is coming – the sun's legs are up in the morning and down in the evening'). If the sun appeared yellow and dull, with heavy clouds near the earth, it meant wet weather. The same was true of a sun that rose cloudy and later appeared gleaming in the presence of a south-westerly wind. A long spell of fine weather could be predicted from a bright sun that appeared to be near the earth, especially if it was combined with a deep blue sky that seemed very far away.

I could go on listing lore about weather signs connected with seals, trees, crops, crickets and the pains in old men's corns, and more of these weather signs and proverbs are listed at the end of this book. I hope that someone will gather all these nuggets and begin the process of researching which of them have most scientific merit. But, for me, what is most precious is the sense of keen observation they reveal. In an era and in a society without access to precise scientific equipment, they reveal how our forebears used heightened observations that are the basis of the scientific method today. They may not have had access to hygrometers or have developed concepts such as isobars, but within the limitations of what was available they were equally intent on analysing and categorising our notoriously complex and unpredictable atmospheric conditions.

And they somehow managed to get a surprising amount right. The lore about how salt melting is a sign of rain is a case in point: it's true that the increased humidity that comes with the low pressure that often precedes rain does cause salt crystals to draw water vapour from the air and to become moist or dissolve. Likewise, a phrase such as *smúr rabharta*, meaning 'the dull weather that accompanies the spring tide', captures a great deal, in that it's an accurate observation of a phenomenon that occurs when the gravitational forces of the moon and the sun align to bring about the highest high tides and the lowest low tides. While this alignment doesn't directly affect cloud cover, when a spring tide coincides with bad weather, severe flooding can occur, making these spring tides more memorable than those that happen in times of fine weather.

*

In an era before weather apps and specialist equipment, sky-watching was more nuanced than it is now. We've all heard the phrase 'A red sky at night is a shepherd's delight', but the gradations used to be more subtle, according to the scholar Dáithí Ó hÓgáin. He writes in his masterful encyclopedia *Myth, Legend & Romance* that a red sky in the east in winter was thought to presage frost or even snow; a red sky to the west meant sunshine; redness in the north predicted rain; and redness in the south meant rain and strong wind. In springtime a red southern sky foretold pleasant moist weather, which would help the crops to grow.

We shouldn't assume that our ancestors relied solely on nature observation for their forecasts. Phil Cronin of the Crossmolina Historical and Folklore Society has related that his mother had a jam jar two-thirds full of water in which she immersed a small Powers whiskey bottle, neck down. 'In fine weather the water moved up a little in the neck of the bottle, and when rain was near it dropped again.' It was a homemade barometer – and an accurate one, too, according to Cronin.

Finally, before we set out on our exploration, let me just touch upon the centrality of weather in our mythological tales, some of which stretch back thousands of years. Storms, floods and sunshine are frequently invoked as elements that precipitate dramatic events in the narratives of the old tales. The Tuatha Dé Danann, a mythical race of semi-divine beings who occupied Ireland before the arrival of our ancestors, were said to have summoned a storm to ward off the first humans to attempt to arrive, and they had themselves arrived by emerging through a dense bank of Otherworldly mist – like a band at a heavy metal concert. This type of mist could allow passage in both directions: in the narrative Imram Brain ('The Voyage of Bran'), Bran and his companions set sail across the Atlantic on an internal and external voyage of discovery and were led to the Otherworld through a veil of heavy mist.

Certain characters are also strongly associated with their ability to influence the weather. The land sovereignty deity An Chailleach ('crone', 'wise woman', 'veiled one') was believed to bring forth the tumultuous storms of early winter as well as the freezing temperatures of midwinter. Manannán mac Lir, a deity associated with the ocean, was known to command mist and sea winds to influence events and impose his will. The god Lugh helped create the conditions for a bountiful harvest, if one was in right relationship to him. In the account of the death of the mythic warrior Cú Chulainn, storms and unnatural darkness are said to have enveloped the land – a sign that the weather was in sympathy with the people.

Fairies were also involved with the creation of weather phenomena. An eerie calm at sea, or a sudden gust of wind, was thought to be caused by the presence of the *daoine maithe* or *sióga* ('good people' or fairies) passing nearby.

There's much more to be said about the role of weather in folklore, and you'll find a few more insights in the weather signs and proverbs in the appendix, but for now let's do a deep dive into the weather words themselves.

RAIN

Ag cur

Raining. It's actually short for *ag cur báistí* (literally, 'putting out with rain'). *Ag cur* also means ploughing, sowing, burying, propelling, setting out, laying down.

Greadadh báistí

A pelting, beating, trouncing rain that drenches you to the skin.

NINETY-NINE WORDS FOR RAIN   12

Lascadh báistí

A rain with wind that lashes, whips and flogs you.

NINETY-NINE WORDS FOR RAIN 14

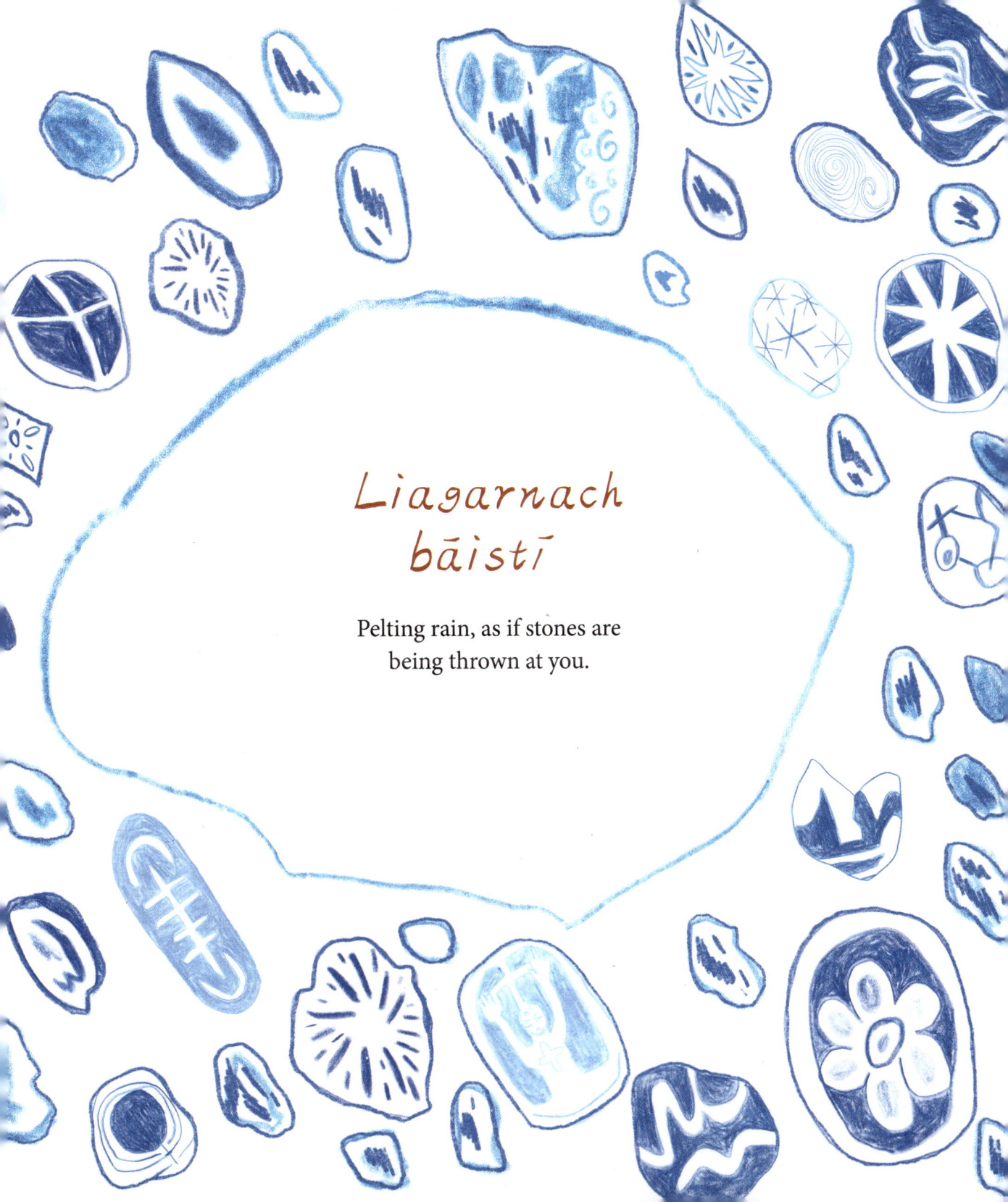

Liagarnach báistí

Pelting rain, as if stones are being thrown at you.

Briodarnach báistí

Raining unpleasantly. *Briodar* means swill, hogwash
or broken, soured milk, conveying the idea of hogwash
or curdled milk falling from the sky.

Caidhleadh báistí

Driving, twisting, coiling rain.

Ragáille báistí

Pelting, tumultuous rain.
Ragáille also means noisy, and in earlier times it meant partying, raucously and drunkenly.

Rilleadh báistí

Streaming rain, like oats through a winnowing sieve.

Dallcairt

Raining so heavily that you cannot see ahead.

Batar fearthainne

A battering, pounding or sudden downpour of rain.

Ag cur dobhar

Raining torrents, or pouring down floods. *Dobhar* is an old word for water, which gives us the word *dobharchú*, an otter (literally, 'water hound'). Nowadays it more often means a flood or torrent. It can also mean darkness and obscurity.

Gleidearnach

Downpour of rain that seems combative or warlike.

Stealladh fearthainne

Spewing, spouting, pouring rain. *Stealladh* can also mean to squabble or argue. *Ag obair ar stealladh* means working at a ferocious pace. *Instealladh* means an injection (literally, 'to pour in').

Báisteach chugainn:
tréad buaibh in aice
le chéile i lár páirce
nach mbeadh fonn
orthu éirí

Rain coming if a herd of cows lie close together in the middle of a field and have no wish to move.

TAOM

Teeming rain. *Taom* refers to straining off water or liquid, such as teeming potatoes, that is, draining the cooking water from them.

Raiste

Rain driven furiously by the wind.

.

Bascadh

A drenching or beating from rain or wind.

Báisteach dheannachtach

Cold, drenching rain. *Deannachtach* means biting, sharp or severe. *Lá deannachtach* means a bitter, nasty day.

Tá sé ag caitheamh sceana gréasaí

Raining heavily
(literally, 'It's throwing cobbler's knives').

NINETY-NINE WORDS FOR RAIN 42

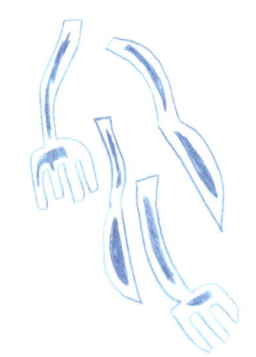

AG CUR
FORC AGUS
SCEANA

Raining forks and knives

Deoir fhearthainne

Raindrop (literally, 'a rain tear').

Ag cur de dhíon is de dheora

Pouring from the roofs and the tears.

An braon anuas

The rain coming through the roof (literally, 'the drop from above'), referring to the water that would seep through a thatch roof in heavy rain, particularly where hens, birds or mice had weakened the tight bundles of straw, reeds or rushes that formed the thatch by making a nest in it. Figuratively, the phrase conveys misfortune and wretchedness.

Mūr bháistí

A heavy fall, or dense wall, of rain.

Fraschith

A heavy shower.

Bailc

A downpour, a heavy shower of rain. *Bailc* also meant bold or strong, and so the great god Balor was known as *Balór Bailc-Bhéimneach* ('Balor of the Mighty Blows'). He rained down punches upon you. A strong thickset man would be described as *bailceach*.

Múrtha péatar

Heavy rain. *Péatar* normally refers to pewter, except in this one case and in the related phrase *Beidh sé 'na phéatar ar ball* ('It'll pour soon'). I have no idea how pewter came to be associated with rain.

Clagarnach

Heavy rain; clattering of heavy rain falling.

Fliuch gaofar is na roilligh ag éagaoin

'Wet and windy when the oystercatchers cry.' Oystercatchers tend to be noisy at all times, but perhaps they call more often before rain. Their shrill, insistent *Peep, peep, peep* is conveyed in Irish as *Bí glic, bí glic* ('Be wise, be prudent'). It was taken as a warning to fishermen of an approaching storm.

Cith toirní

Thundershower.

Duifean

A threat of rain. Darkness, cloudiness, overcast, a scowl.

Bús báistí

Pelting with rain, a rapid hurry of rain.
Bús or *búis* also means a corpulent woman.

Léidearnach chlagair

Pelting, beating rain.

Lá léidearnaí

Wild day of driving rain.

BATHARNACH

Raining in torrents.

Rilleadh

Downpour, torrent, flood.

Báisteach shíobtha

Driving rain. *Síob* was a drift or a gust, driven rain or snow. It also means to hitch a ride.

Má bhíonn an spideog faoi thor ar maidin, beidh sé ina lá fhliuch, ach má bhíonn sí ar an ngéag is airde, is í ag gabhail cheoil, beidh sé ina lá mhaith

'Rain is on the way if the robin hides beneath a bush
at morning time, but if he sings from the highest branch around,
a pleasant day can be expected.'

Síorbháisteach

Persistent rain.

Ag díle báistí

Pouring, flooding with rain. *Díle* originally meant the Biblical flood, from the Latin *diluvium*, which gives us the word 'antediluvian', meaning truly ancient, or before Noah's flood.

Síobadh fearthainne

Lashing, drifting rain.

Spùtrach

Splashing rain, downpour; rain-soaked ground; slush.

NINETY-NINE WORDS FOR RAIN 74

Cáidheach

Dirty, showery, nasty weather. It also means filthy, polluted. The word derives from *cáidhe*, which means filth or obscenity but also holiness, sanctity, chastity.

Síor-chur

The act of continually putting, of doing something or of constantly raining.

Madra ag itheadh féir, tá báisteach air

'A dog eating grass means that it will rain.' This proverb was also recorded in Ontario in the 1930s, and in California. One of those recording the proverb noted that dogs normally eat grass when they have an upset stomach and that the atmospheric change that occurs before a rainstorm might make them experience the symptoms of an upset stomach. It's possible but, in my opinion, this explanation doesn't give enough credence to the intelligence of dogs.

Boglach

Rainy weather; a thaw in snow; saturated ground.

*Ní hé lá na báistí,
lá na bpáistí*

'The rainy day is not the children's day.'

SUDDEN
RAIN

Spairn

Sudden, heavy shower. Also a fight, contention or struggle.

Búisteog

Sudden shower.

Sprais

Heavy, sudden, spattering shower.
It can also refer to a splash of anything.

Liongar ceatha

Heavy shower (literally, 'slimy shower' or 'filthy shower').

Brúisc fearthainne

Sudden fall of rain.

Múirling

Sudden shower. It comes from the word *múr*, which means a shower but also a wall, embankment or rampart, suggesting a sudden bank of rain coming in. *Múr* means a wall in Icelandic too, similar to the French *mur*. They all derive from the Latin *murus* (city wall). It possibly arrived in Ireland as the word for the enclosure around a monastic settlement.

Nuair a bhíonn na seangáin a mbíonn sciatháin orthu amuigh, beidh báisteach air

'When the ants with wings on them are out, it will rain.'

NINETY-NINE WORDS FOR RAIN

Tuile shléibhe

Cloudburst (literally, 'mountain flood'). *Tuile* means flood and gave rise to the expression *Níl tuile dá mhéad nach dtránn* ('No flood is so great that it won't ebb').

Maidhm bháistí

Cloudburst.

Fuarlach

Sudden flooding from heavy rainfall; low-lying marginal land subject to flooding from downpours; weedy, marshy edge of a lake or river.

Scríob báistí

Sudden, violent rain shower.
Scríob means the stress of a coming storm.

Gailfean

Heavy rain, accompanied by strong wind. Rough, blustery weather. It comes from *gaill-shíon*, meaning furious weather.

Bíonn garraí an iascaire
lán le bláthanna bána

'The fisherman's garden is full of white flowers', that is,
there are white horses on the sea. This phrase is one of a number
of examples showing that coastal communities regarded the inner
coastline as part of the land, especially the stretch that extended to the
distance of nine waves, or the general distance that a currach
or naomhóg would travel on a daily fishing trip.

SHOWERS *and* DRIZZLE

Seadbháisteach

Rain in the wind; spitting rain; drizzle.

Cafarnach

Drizzle, from *cafarr*, 'a cap of rain on the landscape',
or a kerchief, a bandage on a head, or a helmet.

Béaltais

Drizzly, damp, soft-lipped, bland. *Béal* means mouth
and *tais* means damp or moist, though it can also mean smooth,
soft and tender, in the sense that our damp climate can make our
skin soft and tender – until the wind comes and withers it!

Draonán

Light rain, drizzle.

Ceobhrán

Light drizzle; mist; haze.

Brádán

Gentle, damp rain; drizzle.

Ceobháisteach

Heavy drizzle; Scotch mist.

Sramach

Drizzly, clammy, damp weather.
Gummy, bleary eyes. Slimy track of a snail.
Clotted traces of blood.

Aimsir chlabach

Murky, muddy weather. *Clabach* means muddy or murky.
It gave rise to the term 'bonny clabber' in Hiberno-English and in
dialects of the southern states of the US. It refers to milk that has
naturally clotted on souring, and its name derives from
bainne clábair ('murky milk').

Nuair a bhíonn an seilide ag snámh ar an dtalamh, beidh báisteach air

'When the snail is sliding on the ground, there will be rain.'

Gailbheach

Windy and showery. A slight misty shower.
Blustery, stormy rain. Also, peevish, testy, angry.

Scráib

A short, sharp, blustery shower. *Scráib* means a scrape or a scratch, suggesting that the rain is not quite as wounding as a full drenching downpour.

Breacbháisteach

Occasional rain. *Breac* is a powerful and mysterious word. It means speckled, dappled or occasional and can also imply magical abilities, such as being able to pass between physical dimensions, though *breacbháisteach* is unlikely to have any occult qualities.

Fras

A shower. It can refer to a shower of tears, blood, seeds or stones, but most often rain.

Frasach

Showery. Raining, pouring. Generous, fruitful, copious.

Gailbh

Windy shower.

Srathach

Showery, layered, tiered.

Cith gealáin

Sunny shower.

Múirín gréine

Sun shower.

Craobhmhúr

Scattered rain. *Craobh* means the branch of a tree or a branch of a plant or animal family. I like to think that the word *craobhmhúr* regards this 'scattered' rain as the offspring of a heavier downpour elsewhere. There's another rain expression that uses *craobh*: *Tá craobh fhliuch ar an lá*, which means that it's likely to rain today but is literally 'There's a wet branch on the day', as though the day is seeded from the phenomenon, or the family, of rain.

Lá béalcheathach

Day of wind-blown showers; drizzly day.

Duifean mór ar bheagán fearthainne

Much cloud bringing little rain; much ado about nothing. *Duifean* means cloudiness, darkness, gloom, melancholy. It's one of the many Irish words that derive from *dubh*, meaning black or dark.

Salachar

Drizzle, smattering of rain. From *salach* ('dirty').

Drothán

Drizzle.

Fliuchbháisteach

Drizzle.

Siobráil

Mist, drizzle.

Sreangán ceo

Band of drizzly mist.

BÉALFHLIUCH

Drizzling (literally, 'wet-mouthed'). It can also refer to someone who's fond of a drink.

Ceathán

Light shower.

Frasú

Showering.

Ceathannach

Showery.

Crithnéal

A shower (literally, 'shaking cloud').

Gruamán

Gloomy spell of weather; fit of despondency.

Braoille fearthainne

A heavy shower of rain. *Braoille*, meaning crack or clap, suggests a sudden and thunderous shower.

SCRABHA

A passing shower, a dark cloud.

Nuair bhíonn an ghlasóg ag teacht go dtí an doras, tá drochaimsir ag teacht

'When the wagtail comes to the door, bad weather is approaching.'

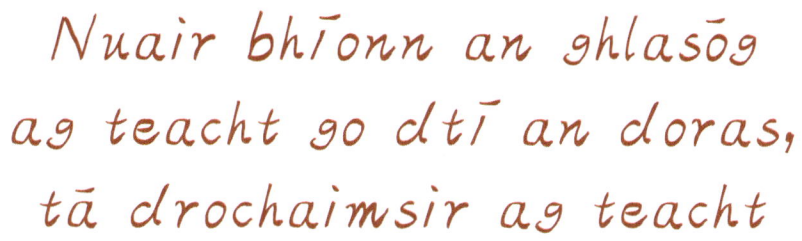

Múrail

Act of descending in showers; showery conditions.

Sriabhán

Heavy mist, drizzle. *Sriabhán* is possibly connected with *sreabhán,* a streamlet, from *sreabh*, a drip, drop or flow – often used to refer to milk from a cow's teat. The phrase *Níl sreabh aici* means 'She doesn't have a drop', as in 'She's not giving any milk'.

TONNCHITH

A violent shower (literally, 'wave-shower').

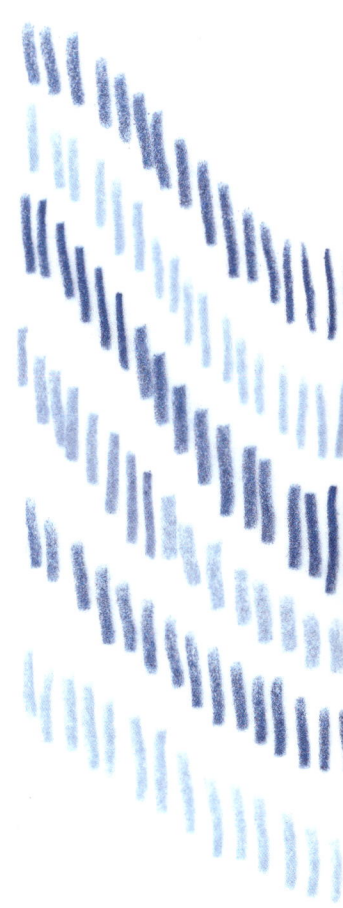

A LULL
in the RAIN

Turadh

Cessation of rain, from *tur* ('dry', 'arid', 'without relish'). I love the expression *Ní thiocfaimid tur as a theach*, meaning 'We won't come dry from his house', that is, 'He'll surely serve us food and drink'.

Sánas

A lull in a rainstorm.

Beach ag saothar
agus an ghrian faoi –
athrú aimsire

'The bee working after sunset – a change in the weather.'

Aiteall

Fine spell between showers. Joy, cheerfulness.

Brŭchtadh

The sudden appearance of the sun after rain.
It also means bursting, pouring out, gushing forth … or belching.

Ag spalpadh suas

Clearing up (after rain), from *spalp*, to burst forth,
gush out or beat down. *Spalpadh gréine* means a burst of sunshine.

Lig an bháisteach fúithi

The rain lightened (literally, 'The rain let from under her').

Fáfall fearthainne

The easing off of rain after a downpour. *Fáfall* seems to be a variation of *támhall*, 'calm, sheltered waters'. It relates to the tranquil, safer waters that a fisherman enters when approaching the coastline from the wilder ocean.

Cothromacan síne na haimsire

The tendency of good and bad spells of weather to offset each other over a period. It literally means 'The balancing or equalisation of one form of weather with another'. The phrase was often uttered in exasperation after a long, bleak, dreary spell of bad weather, spoken in the belief that there would have to come a time of equally fine weather. Alas, it's not necessarily true, as another expression makes clear: *Ná creid Fionn is ná creid Fiach, is ná creid briathartha mná, mar más moch mall a éireos an ghrian, is mar is toil le Dia a bheas an lá* ('Don't believe Fionn and don't believe Fiach, and don't believe women's words, as just as certain as the sun rises, it's God's decision how the day will be').

MIST

Ceo

Fog, mist, haze.

Drúnsaoth

Light mist.

Fionncheo

Light mist, bright mist.

Scamallaigh
Cloud (over), mist, obscure.

CIACHMHAR

Misty, foggy, gloomy, obscure; sad, melancholy.

Scim

Veil of mist, a haze; a magical vision;
a fairy film over the land, denoting prosperity;
succumbing to the supernatural world through sleep.

Smúit

Mist, murkiness. Also, smoke and vapour.

Smúitcheo

Dense mist.

Doilbhcheo

Dark, deceptive mist.

Caifirín ceo

Head shawl or cap of mist. Also, *cáipín ceo*, a hat of mist.

Chomh sean leis an gceo

As old as the mist.

Chomh liath leis an gceo

As grey as the mist – a way of expressing that someone or something is truly ancient.

Cuisne

A frost mist, a fog in frosty weather.

Daillchiach

A blind mist, a heavy sadness. *Ciach* is an alternative genitive to *ceo*, mist. The expression *Cobha ciach a chur ar dhuine* means to befog or confuse someone. *Cobha* means misty vision, from cataracts or hardening of the eyeballs, so the expression means 'to put the mist of the mistiness of vision on someone'.

Geimhreadh ceoch, earrach reoch, samhradh grianmhar, is fómhar breá biamhar

A misty winter, a frosty spring, a sunny summer and a fine, fruitful autumn. These were considered to be the ideal qualities for each season to ensure a bountiful harvest in autumn. Interestingly, it's winter that's misty and spring that's frosty, rather than the other way round. Snow is not mentioned, as it was not common along the west coast, where these Irish phrases lasted longest.

Ceo sí

Fairy mist. A mist that could descend without warning, disorienting a person and perhaps heralding their death. Also known as *ceo draíochta* (literally, 'magic mist').

RAINBOWS

Bogha báistí

Bow of rain.

Bogha síne

Bow of weather.

Tuar ceatha

A rainbow (literally, 'omen, precursor or prophecy of rain').

Stua ceatha

(Literally, 'shower arch'.) *Stua* means not only an arc or arch but also, by extension, a stately person or warrior. It gave rise to the word *stuaire*, which describes a woman of the highest calibre.

Léas doininne

Rainbow, light near the horizon portending a storm.
Literally, 'ray of light of bad weather'.

NINETY-NINE WORDS FOR RAIN   200

Madra gaoithe

Rainbow, light over the horizon portending a storm. Literally, 'dog of the wind'.

Breaclá

Day of sun and showers.

SUN

AN GHRIAN

The sun.

That's it, I'm afraid: there really is only one word for sun in Irish. Make of that what you will. There are words for how the sun shines, and sets, and rises, but *an ghrian* is the full extent of Irish words for sun.

SUN WORDS

Spalp

Burst forth.

Gealānach

Gleaming, flashing.

Ruithneach

Gleaming, radiant, sparkly, from the verb *ruithnigh*, to make radiant, to brighten, to illuminate.

Glé

Luminous.

Soilseach

Luminescent.

Solasmhar

Sunlit, bright, luminous.

Sorcha

Bright.

Gléineach

Vivid, bright.

Gluair

Bright, clear, harsh.

Greadánach

Bright, intense. It also means fighting, a hullaballoo or a stinging pain, and it can be used to refer to rain that beats down. *An fhearthainn ag greadadh ar na crainn* ('The rain whipping the trees').

Greadhnach

Blazing, bright. It usually refers to a merry, cheerful person or to a bright, blazing fire or sun.

Niamhrach

Splendid, bright, radiant. It comes from *niamh*, meaning brightness, lustre, brilliance. *Niamh óir* is the sheen of gold, and *niamh na gréine* is the sun's incandescence. Hence the name Niamh.

Trilseach

Glittering, bright. It comes from *trilis* and *trilseán*, which mean a plaited rushlight, a torch or hair tresses.

TROIGHEAN

The redness of the rising sun;
the pith or resin of pinewood.

Fáinne geal an lae

Sunrise (literally, 'bright ring of day').

Breacadh an lae

Sunrise (literally, 'brightening of the day').

Bánú an lae

Sunrise (literally, 'whitening of the day').

Súil an lae

Sunrise (literally, 'eye of the day').

Éirí na gréine

Rising of the sun.

Troighean ghréine

Rising of the sun. *Troighean*, as mentioned earlier, refers to the redness of the rising sun, and as such this expression is similar to *deargadh na gréine* ('reddening of the sun'), which is another term for sunrise. *Troighean* often refers to fish oil, or a greasy, smudgy substance, or the dark reddish sap emitted from pine. Interestingly, *troighean sneachta* means a covering of (melting) snow. Go figure!

Turgbháil na gréine

Sunrise, the ascending of the sun in the heavens.

Tá Mór 'na suí

The sun is up (literally, 'Mór has risen', Mór being a pagan goddess from Munster known as *Mór Mumhan* and initially as *Mór-Ríoghain*). *Mór* is still used instead of *Dia* (God) in some salutations: *Mór dhuit* ('The blessings of Mór to you'), *Mór do bheatha* ('May Mór give you health'), *Mór is Muire is Pádraig dhuit* ('The blessings of Mór, Mary and St Patrick to you').

Drithligh

Sparkle, scintillate.

Spréach

Sparkle, spark, spirit, animated life force.

Ruithnigh

Make radiant, brighten.

Saighneáil

Shine.

Scal

Flash.

Grianda

Solar.

Drithle

A drop glancing in the sun; a sparkle, a twinkle; a glimpse.

Grianbhuí

Golden sunlight, the peculiar colour of sunset in summer.

AG GLIOSCARNACH

Twinkling, glistening.

Breacshoilsigh

Glimmer.

Crithlonraigh

Shimmer.

Dallraigh

Glare.

Breoigh
Glow.

Dealraigh
Gleam, shine forth.

Gathaigh
Radiate.

Lonrach
Radiant.

Ionsoilsigh

Illuminate.

Sorchaigh

Illuminate, enlighten. From *sorcha* ('brightness, light, cheerfulness'). It's the opposite of *dorcha* ('darkness'), as seen in the expression *An Té a rinne sorcha agus dorcha*, 'He who made light and darkness, day and night'. There are a number of pairs of words in Irish in which the positive attribute begins with an S, and its negative opposite is the same word, but with the S replaced by a D, as in *soineann* 'fine weather' and *doineann* 'foul weather'.

Fad is a bheidh an ghrian ag dul deiseal

'As long as the sun is turning sunwise', an expression that refers to forever, till the end of time.

Thugamar an ghrian abhaile linn

We got home before dark (literally, 'We brought the sun home with us').

Faoithin

Sundown, eventide. *Ó mhaidin go faoithin*
('from dawn till sunset')

Luí gréine

Sunset (literally, 'the lying down of the sun').

Dul faoi na gréine

Sunset (literally, 'the going under of the sun').

Fuineadh gréine

Sunset (literally, 'the finishing or conclusion of the sun'); *ó thurgbháil go fuineadh* ('from sunrise to sunset').

Tiocfaidh lá fós a mbeidh gnó ag an mbó dá heireaball

'The day will still come when that cow needs its tail', meaning that good weather could still come this year.

Conclusion

AS WE MOVE forward in a world that depends increasingly on polar-orbiting and geostationary satellites, Doppler radar and supercomputers running complex numerical weather models to predict our weather, it's worth reflecting on what should be done with all these old insights. Certainly, weather words and lore can appear outmoded at times, but there is still enormous value in these traditions and customs as a remnant of our ancestral inheritance, if only as a testament to the observational ability of those who preceded us and their creativity in communicating complex weather patterns in simple, engaging words and phrases. They can help us observe and interpret our environment in more considered ways. Over time, this can help to foster a deeper connection with nature.

Some weather lore is location-specific, reflecting regional climate patterns that may not be captured by broader forecasting models. The people of Clifden don't need to tune in to Met Éireann to know whether it will rain if they see fog on the top of Errisbeg Hill or if the sea is heard roaring around Carraig na Rón.

And, more generally, many weather sayings, particularly those based on observable natural phenomena, remain reliable for predicting short-term weather changes. If the battery suddenly dies on your phone when you're out hiking, or a satellite malfunctions when you're at sea, it can be useful to know that the curlews calling presage rain, that shining mackerel means rough seas or that flatfish on the surface signals a storm.

These, after all, are the nuggets of wisdom that have kept us safe and informed for countless generations – part of the amassed knowledge of the humans who have so long occupied this island. It would be rash to discard them too quickly.

There's no denying that modern meteorology has outstripped the old customs in accuracy and scope, but I, for one, want to live in a world where I can gauge the rain not by checking a weather app on my phone but by the presence of a leprechaun of the ditch in my kitchen, which is what my granduncle used to say: *Déanfaidh sé báisteach throm má thagann leipreachán an chlaí isteach sa chistin*: 'It will rain hard if a leprechaun of the ditch comes into the kitchen.' A *leipreachán an chlaí* was a colloquial term for a frog.

Here's hoping we can find a way to preserve these precious aspects of our inheritance. It can be done, as the phrase goes, *Le cúnamh Dé agus na dea-uaine*: 'With the help of God and fine weather.'

Appendix

Weather Signs from the Aran Islands: From the Schools' Collection

Auguries of good weather
Nuair a bhíonn an liamhán i ngar don talamh: 'When the basking shark is near land.'
Nuair a thagann na faoileáin isteach ar an dtalamh: 'When the seagulls come in on the land.'
Nuair a bhíonn na muca mara ag éirí ar bharr na farraige: 'When the porpoises rise to the surface.'
Nuair a théann na géanna fiana ó dheas: 'When the wild geese fly south.'
Nuair a bhíonn an talamh ó dheas agus ó thuaidh i bhfad amach: 'When the land to the south and north appears far away.'

Auguries of rain
Taoille mhór a bheith ann: 'A flood tide.'
Eascainn a bheith i bhfior-uisce: 'Eels being in fresh water.'
Fáinne a bheith timpeall ar an ngealach: 'A ring surrounding the moon.'

Auguries of general bad weather
Na faoileáin ar an bhfarraige: 'The seagulls being out at sea.'
Na héisc ag imeacht amach san fharraige: 'The fish heading out to sea.'
Na faoileáin ag teacht aníos ag piocadh ar an bhféar: 'The seagulls coming down to pick at the grass.'
Na muca mara ag dul amach i bhfad ins an bhfarraige: 'The porpoises heading far out to sea.'
Na réalta a bheith i ngar don ghealach: 'The stars appearing close to the moon.'

Further bad weather signs, according to Nuala Seóigeach of Cill Éinne on Inis Mór
Madra uisce a fheiceáil ag siúl ar thalamh tirim: 'Seeing an otter walking on dry land.'
An gobadán ag imeacht ar an trá: 'The sandpiper out on the strand.'

Another Aran Island source
Nuair a bhíonn sléibhte Chiarraí le feiceáil i ngar dúinn bíonn drochaimsir air: 'When the Kerry mountains appear close, bad weather will follow.'
Bíonn cuilleoga, míoltóga agus cleabhair chaocha ag imeacht go fairsing le linn báistí, go mór mhór sa samhradh: 'Flies, midges and warble flies are widespread during rain, especially in summer.'
Tagann dath uaithne ar an ngríosaigh roimh báistí: 'The embers turn green before rain.'
Nuair atá dath gorm ar an ngríosach tá athrú aimsire ag teacht: 'When the embers are blue the weather will change.'

Nuair a bhíonn deatach na tine ar fud an tí, tá athrú aimsire ag teacht: 'When the smoke fills the house, the weather will change.'

Tagann athrú ar an aimsir in-éadan gach ceathrú don ghealaigh: 'Weather changes at the end of every quarter moon.'

Má bhíonn drochaimsir ann le tús gealaí nua is iondúil go mbeidh sé garbh go mbeidh ceathrú den ghealach ann: 'Bad weather at a new moon means it will likely remain rough until its first quarter.'

Nuair a bhíonn ballaí an tí fuar fliuch sin cosúlacht báistí: 'When the walls are cold and wet it's a sign of rain.'

An ghaoth a fhágann an tSamhain againn, sin í an ghaoth is mó a beidh againn ar feadh na bliana: 'The November wind will be the worst of the year.'

Cé ar bith sórt aimsire a bhíonn ann an Déardaoin deiridh den ghealach, sin í an aimsir a beidh againn nuair a thagann an ghealach nua: 'Whatever weather we have on the last Thursday of the moon, that'll be the weather we have when the new moon comes.'

Bíonn Dé hAoine in aghaidh na seachtaine: má bhíonn chuile lá eile breá bíonn an Aoine go h-olc, agus bíonn an Aoine breá nuair a bhíonn na laethanta eile go holc: 'Friday goes against the week: if every other day is fine, Friday will be bad, and Friday is fine when the other days are bad.'

Nuair a thosnaíonn sé ag báisteach tús Aoine, nó deireadh Sathairn, ní éiríonn sé as an lá sin: 'When it starts raining early on a Friday, or late on a Saturday, it will continue all day.'

Proverbs

SEANFHOCAIL ('OLD SAYINGS') are pithy and often poetic phrases that encapsulate wisdom and observations about life in a preliterate society. They tend to provide concise, well-wrought insights into life and nature – a brief string of words that can be picked apart to reveal hidden dimensions of metaphor and meaning about social values, natural phenomena and universal human experience. At their best, they can approach the expansiveness, elusiveness and multilayered nuance of a koan.

The *seanfhocail* listed here repeat some of the insights in the weather lore section but more eloquently. Taken as a whole, they reveal at least as much about our traditional knowledge of, and attitude to, weather as all the previous pages.

Deireadh ceatha ceo, is deireadh ceo gaoth: 'Mist banishes rain, and wind banishes mist.'

Tosach ceatha ceo: 'Mist precedes rain.'

Ceo soininne ar aibhneacha, ceo doininne ar chnoic: 'Mist of good weather on rivers, mist of bad weather on hills.'

Fearthainn do ghamhain, is gaoth do shearrach, uisce do ghé, is déirc do bhacach: 'Rain for a calf, and wind for a foal, water for a goose, and charity for the lame.'

Mar a ligfeá trí chriathar é: 'As if you let it through a sieve.' (Said about heavy rain.)

An ghaoth aduaidh, bíonn sí crua agus cuireann sí fuacht ar dhaoine: 'The north wind is severe and makes people cold.'

An ghaoth aneas, bíonn sí tais agus cuireann sí duilleoga ar chrainnte: 'The south wind is damp and puts leaves on trees.'

An ghaoth anoir, bíonn sí géar agus cuireann sí gruaim ar chaoirigh: 'The east wind is sharp and makes sheep sombre.'

An ghaoth aniar, bíonn sí fial agus cuireann sí iasc i líonta: 'The west wind is bountiful and puts fish in nets.'

Is gnách don ghaoth mhór fearthainn a bheith ina dhiaidh: 'Rain usually follows a big storm.'

Má lagaíonn an ghaoth anuas ar fad, bí ag súil aneas ansin léi, agus báisteach lena cois: 'If the wind calms entirely, expect her from the south, and rain to follow.'

Tá an ghaoth anoir is an fhearthainn aniar air: 'The wind is to the east and the rain to the west of him' (that is, everything has gone awry with him).

Má ghlaonn an chuach ar chrann gan duilliúr, díol do bhó agus ceannaigh arbhar: 'If the cuckoo sings on a leafless tree, sell your cow and buy corn.'

Doineann má bhíonn cúr ar bhóithríní bána tríd an bhfarraige: 'Bad weather when there is foam on the white roads through the sea.'

Garbhadas amárach má bhíonn go leor cúir in aice an chósta, lán mara: 'Rough weather tomorrow if there is a lot of foam near the coast at high tide.'

Olc síon an sioc. Is fearr sioc ná sneachta. Agus is fearr sneachta ná síorbháisteach: 'Frost is bad weather. Frost beats snow. Snow beats constant rain.'

Fógraíonn fáinleoga ísle doineann: 'Low-flying swallows portend bad weather.'

Márta crua gaofar agus Aibreán bog braonach – chun torthaí a thabhairt: 'A hard windy March and a soft, wet April – for fruitful yields.'

Is iomaí athrú a chuireann lá Márta de: 'A March day has many changes.'

Bíonn srón dubh ar gach maidin earraigh, agus eireaball searraigh as san siar: 'Every spring morning has a black nose and a foal's tail from then on.'

Laethanta na Bó Riabhaí: 'Days of the speckled cow.' (This refers to a period at the end of March and beginning of April. The old cow had managed to survive through the perishing March days, but then March lent some of its days to April, which killed off the poor cow.)

Scairbhín/Garbhshíon na gCuach: 'The rough weather of the cuckoo.' (This refers to a period at the end of April that can be wintry.)

PROVERBS 251

Praise for Manchán Magan

'If you're into Irish mythology, Manchán has got some incredibly interesting theories ... and he's got some theories about the roots of the Irish language that are going to blow your head off'.
Blindboy Boatclub

'One only needs to wade a few pages into this rich and absorbing work (*Thirty-Two Words for Field*) to see that perhaps we could do with a lot more characters like Manchán Magan dotted about this world.'
Hilary A. White, *Irish Independent*

'*Thirty-Two Words for Field* … blew open the doors for readers who were keen to connect with the language but lacked access points.'
The Irish Times

'*Thirty-Two Words for Field* has had a huge impact on people throughout the pandemic. That reflects a surge in interest in the Irish language, which is no accident. It goes back to that need for connection.'
Irish Independent